25 SPOOKY DEEP SEA CREATURES

SELENA DALE

25 SPOOKY DEEP SEA CREATURES

BOOK 9

Selena Dale

HERE'S YOUR SPECIAL **Bonus**

Just to say thank you for purchasing this book, I want to give you 2 free coloring books.

TO GET YOUR FREE GIFTS

CLICK THE LINK AT THE END OF THIS BOOK

Table of Contents

Introduction

Our world is a very big place covered by land and water. In fact, the surface of the planet is approximately 71% water. That means most of our planet, Earth, is covered in water!

It contains five oceans, including the Arctic, Atlantic, Indian, Pacific and Southern. We know there are animals that live in these oceans including a whole variety of fish. We also know that the oceans are very deep...but there is only so far we humans can go to explore.

Lots of life exists in much of the oceans around us but we often do not think about the creatures that live deep, deep, deep below the surface. Some creatures live so deep down that the area around them is total darkness.
What types of creatures lurk at these deep depths? The answers may surprise you!

Scientists are working hard to explore the deep sea with special marine robots and strong diving subs. Over the years they have discovered new and amazing creatures that may shock you to look at them.

Exploration has led to finding new creatures never seen by humans before many of which look very strange. Some look funny and others look scary and spooky.

Ok, it is time for you to put on your explorer's hat and discover some of the weirdest looking ocean creatures you will ever see!

1. DEEP SEA DRAGONFISH

The Deep Sea Dragonfish is a ferocious predator with extremely large teeth. It looks like a big fish but in fact it is only around 6 inches in length, (just a bit longer than a pencil).

It has a long protrusion attached to its chin that produces its own flashing lights. By flashing it on and off and waving it around it can disorient and attract the attention of its potential meal.

A curious fish will get close to the lights for a better look and before it can swim away it is snapped up in the Dragonfish's powerful jaws. It feeds on small fish and crustaceans as well as anything else it can find.

The Dragonfish lives in deep ocean waters at depths of up to 5,000 feet, (1,500 meters). The Deep Sea Dragonfish is found mainly in the North and Western Atlantic Ocean and the Gulf of Mexico

2. DEEP SEA ANGLERFISH

Just like the Dragonfish, the Deep Sea Anglerfish uses light to catch its prey. It has a long protrusion attached to its head that flashes a blue-green light to attract the attention of any fish nearby.

When its prey gets close enough, the Anglerfish snaps it up and swallows it whole. It isn't fussy about what it eats and tends to have a lot of success catching small squid.

The Anglerfish is a small fish, reaching up to around 5 inches in length and has a very large mouth with sharp, fang-like teeth. It has a big round body so it doesn't swim very fast.

It lives in total darkness at depths of up to a mile below sea level, in an area called "the midnight zone."

3. FANGTOOTH

The Fangtooth lives in many of the deepest tropical oceans around the world including Australia. It has very sharp, pointy teeth which are actually the largest teeth of any fish in the ocean when taken in proportion to body size. These teeth are useful for biting into squid or other small fish.

It looks like a monster but is actually a small fish, at a length of only 6 inches, (16 centimeters). It has a short, deep body and a large head and mouth.

It has very poor eyesight due to its small eyes but compensates for that by being able to sense movement and vibration in the surrounding water.

The Fangtooth is one of the deepest living fish species and are commonly seen as deep as 6,500 feet, (2,000 meters). Some go as deep as 16,000 feet, (5,000 meters).

4. GULPER EEL

The Gulper Eel has an enormous mouth that is much larger than its body. Its jaw is loosely hinged and can be opened wide enough to swallow an animal much larger than itself.

It has very small eyes and a very long, whip-like tail. The eel uses its tail to move and also for attracting small fish by flashing a pink and red light attached to the end.

When small fish are in range, the eel lunges and snaps them up in its gigantic mouth. Its diet consists mainly of small crustaceans and squid.

The Gulper Eel can vary in length from 3 to 6 feet, (about 1 to 2 meters) and is found in all of the world's tropical oceans. It can swim down to depths of 6,000 feet, (1,800 meters).

5. OARFISH

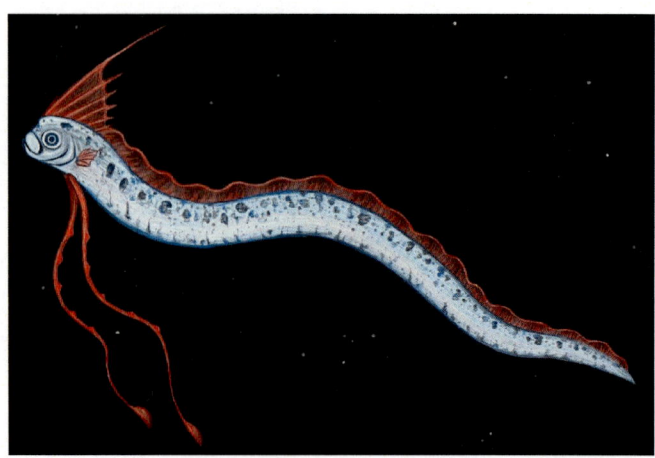

The Oarfish is the longest bony fish in the sea. These creatures have a habit of floating near the surface of the water when they are sick or dying and sometimes wash ashore on beaches after big storms.

They are very long with a slim body that can reach over 50 feet, (15 meters) and weigh up to 600 pounds, (272 kilograms). Their dorsal fin runs the entire length of the fish and has over 400 tiny individual spines projecting out.

They have a small mouth with no visible teeth and they eat small fish, small crustaceans and small squid.

Oarfish are found throughout the deep seas of the Atlantic Ocean and Mediterranean Sea. They can swim as deep as 600 feet, (200 meters) and some can go as deep as 3,000 feet, (1,000 meters).

6. GIANT SQUID

The Giant Squid is one of the world's largest creatures in the sea. It is known to reach a length of up to 60 feet.

It has a main body, eight arms, and two longer tentacles. It also has huge eyes the size of an average dinner plate. The inside surfaces of the tentacles are lined with hundreds of suction cups and each cup is surrounded by sharp edges that help the squid hold on to its prey. They feed on all kinds of fish and other species of squid.

The Giant Squid can move through the water quickly by taking water into its body and then expelling it with great force like jet propulsion.

They are found in all the world's oceans at depths of 2,000 feet, (600 meters).

7. VIPERFISH

The viperfish is one of the fiercest predators of the deep. It has a large mouth and sharp, fang-like teeth. The fangs are so large that they will not fit inside the mouth. It uses its teeth to impale other fish by swimming at them fast.

A long dorsal spine sticks out of its back that flashes light at the tip. It uses this light to attract its prey by flashing it on and off.

The viperfish is a small creature, growing to about 12 inches, (30 centimeters) in length. They have a hinged skull, used for swallowing large fish. They mostly feed on crustaceans and small fish although they can go for days without food.

They can be found in deep water down to 5,000 feet, (1,500 meters).

8. VAMPIRE SQUID

The Vampire Squid looks more like a jellyfish than the common squid. It is a small creature, growing to only about 6 inches in length. It has large fins at the top of its body that look like funny ears. By flapping those fins the squid can push itself through the water real fast.

It has 8 arms that are connected with a webbing of skin. As a defence, the squid can pull its arms up over itself to covers its body in a web.

The Vampire Squid's body can glow in the dark and it can "turn itself on or off" at will. When it turns off it will be completely invisible in the dark waters.

It eats prawns and other small invertebrates and is found in the deep oceans of the tropical world. They can go as deep as 3,000 feet, (over 900 meters).

9. DEEP SEA HATCHETFISH

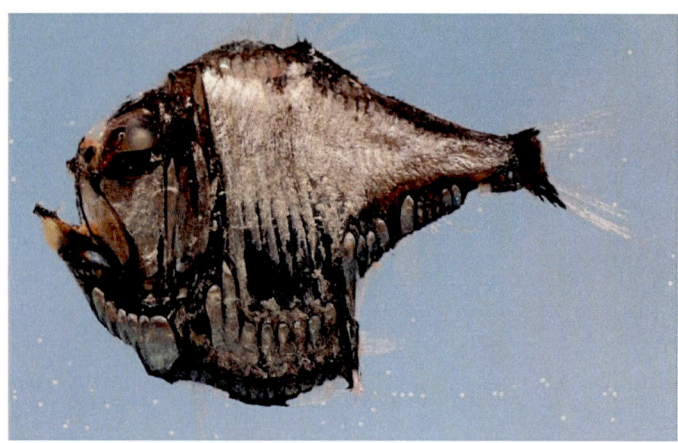

There are about 45 individual species of Hatchet fish with the biggest being 6 inches, (12 centimeters) in length. They have very thin bodies and from the side they resemble the blade of a hatchet.

Hatchet fish feed mainly on plankton and tiny fish. They have large eyes that point upward that enables them to search for food falling from above.

Like many other deep sea fish, the Hatchet fish can light up areas of its body to help catch prey and also to hide from predators. It can adjust the intensity of the lights on their belly to make them seem invisible against the faint light on the ocean surface.

Hatchet fish are found in most temperate waters of the world and can swim as deep as 4,500 feet, (1,370 meters).

10 COFFINFISH

The Coffin fish looks a little like a pink balloon floating in the water. It will inflate its body with air, making itself appear bigger to keep predators away. Its maximum body length is roughly 8.7 inches, (22 cm).

Its body is covered in tiny spines and it also has a small lure that sticks out between its eyes. The end of this lure will flash a light to attract prey. When the lure is not in use the Coffin fish will tuck it back into a small groove on its snout.

This fish spends much of its time lying silently on the ocean floor. It can go as deep as 1000 ft, (305 meters).

Most Coffin fish can be found off the east coast of Australia.

11. BLUE-RINGED OCTOPUS

The Blue-Ringed Octopus is one of the most deadly of all octopuses and there are at least ten different species of them. They have eight arms all with two rows of suction cups, a very big head and two huge eyes.

These octopuses may be deadly but they are not as big as you may think. In fact they are small enough to fit into the palm of your hand.

The blue rings on their body begin to flash when the octopus thinks it is in danger. It is a sort of warning to keep other creatures away.

The Blue-Ringed Octopus eats small crustaceans such as shrimp, crabs, and small fish and can be found all over Australia, New Guinea, Indonesia, Philippines, Malaysia and Japan.

12. GIANT SPIDER CRAB

The Giant Spider Crab, also known as the Japanese Spider, is one of the world's biggest crabs. It is also one of the longest living creatures and can survive for up to 100 years.

These crabs can have a leg span of 12 feet and can weigh up to 43 pounds. They have eight long legs and two long arms with powerful claws on the end.

Giant Spider Crabs spend most of their time at the bottom of the ocean and can eat anything smaller than they are. This includes fish, algae and many other plants. They tend to do a lot of scavenging too.

These creatures are very much at home in the deep, dark depths of the ocean and can be found as deep as 1000 feet. They will only be found in Japan.

13. BARRELEYE FISH

The Barreleye fish is a very strange looking creature. It is named after its eyes because they are shaped like barrels.

The fish has a completely transparent, fluid-filled dome on its head. Yes, you can see inside its head! Its eyes look through the transparent dome, rotated forward or straight up.

It has a tiny mouth and its body is covered with large scales. Its length is around 44cm so it's not a very big fish. Large, flat fins help it to stay motionless in the water in a horizontal position while its eyes looking upward.

The Barreleye fish can be found at depths of at least 800 metres, (2,600 ft) and lives in the North Pacific oceans.
It eats jellyfish, small fish and other crustacean prey.

14. GRENADIER

The Grenadier is a long Eel-like fish that has huge eyes, a huge head and a long fin at the end.

It uses a special light on its underside to shine in different directions. It uses this as a kind of spotlight to see the floor beneath where there might be food.

Grenadiers can also sense movement and vibrations in the water around them. These sensors will help it locate food in the total darkness of the deep sea.

The Grenadier will hover around the sea bed in search of food and sometimes it will sift through the mud with its snout to find worms and other tiny creatures.

It is quite a long fish reaching lengths of up to 1.5 meters and lives deep in the sea at depths of up to 6,000 meters, (20,000 ft).

15. DUMBO OCTOPUS

The Dumbo Octopus may be one of the cutest looking creatures that live in the deep sea. It is named after the Disney cartoon character Dumbo the elephant because of its floppy ear-like fins.

There are 37 different species of Dumbo octopuses all of which can be found in many worldwide oceans. Most are quite small at only 8 inches in length but some can be as big as a few feet.

The octopus has a soft oval-shaped body with 8 arms. The 2 ear-like fins are on both sides of the "head". Its arms have small harpoon-like barbs that will latch onto prey when it is caught.

It lives on the sea bed at a depth of around 23 000 feet and eats different crustaceans, worms and other tiny creatures. The Dumbo Octopus can live up to 5 years.

16. BLACK SWALLOWER

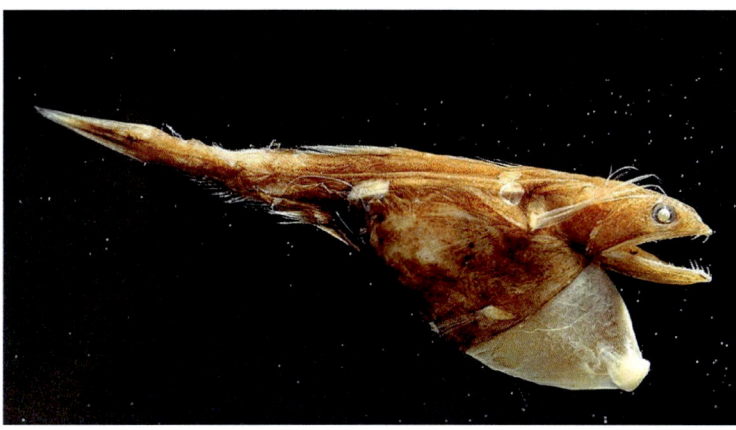

The Black Swallower is a pretty small fish at up to 25 cm, (10 inches) long, but it is able to "swallow" creatures bigger and heavier than itself.

When it does this its stomach will stretch so much that it goes transparent. Yes, you can actually see what it is eating!

These greedy creatures will grab its prey by the tail and slowly force it whole into its stomach. It uses its hooked front teeth to push its prey into its mouth. As it does this the stomach grows and becomes increasingly grotesque.

Black Swallowers can swim in depths between 700 and 2,745 meters, (2,300-9,000 ft). It eats all kinds of fish, and whatever else fits in its mouth, and prefers to live in tropical oceans in the north and south-western Atlantic Ocean.

17. FANFIN SEA DEVIL

The Fanfan Seadevil is a fairly ugly deep sea creature that looks like it belongs in a horror movie. It is from the Anglerfish family and has a round body, fan-like fins, very small eyes and a big mouth filled with sharp teeth.

The fish is mostly black which makes it very difficult to spot in the deep dark ocean. This works to its advantage because being hidden in the dark allows it to get closer to its prey.

Female Fanfin Seadevils are much bigger than males. Males can only grow to about 1 inch in length while the females can grow up to about 8 inches.

The females have a sort of flashing light fishing pole on their head. That pole is used to attract prey in the darkness of the deep sea.

18. FROGFISH

Frogfish have over 45 species at sizes from 5 to 40cm. They hang from corals and sponges while they wait for their prey.

Just like Anglerfish, these fish have a rod and lure used to attract prey. These can be different shapes such as twigs, worms and feathers in order bait a potential meal.

Frogfish have no teeth but use a powerful suction to catch its meal. It can swallow prey up to twice their own size. They eat small crustaceans, fish and tiny Eels.

Frogfish prefer to walk on twos and fours! They have leg-like fins with webbed feet that they use to move about.

Deep sea Frogfish live in waters as deep as 4000 meters and can be found in tropic and sub-tropic areas of the world.

19. LIONFISH

The Lionfish is probably one of the more beautiful deep sea fish but do not let its colorful appearance fool you. This fish is poisonous to all that touch it.

It has 18 needle-like dorsal fins that all have poison tips. A sting from a Lionfish would be very painful to humans but is not powerful enough to kill.

The Lionfish uses fast reflexes to capture its prey. It also spreads its many fins to herd tiny fish into one area where it can more easily swallow them. It mostly eats fish and shrimp.

These fish grow to about 1 foot in length but there are a few that grow even bigger reaching lengths of 15 inches. They can live to around 16 years in the wild and often live longer when looked after by humans in giant aquariums.

20. YETI CRAB

The Yeti Crab is a strange deep sea creature that seems to be totally blind. It was discovered in 2005 on the Pacific Ocean floor as deep as 7200 feet.

It is approximately 15 cm, (5.9 in) long and has legs and claws that are covered with long yellow hairs. In amongst these hairs are tiny bacteria that the crab actually "grows" so that it can feed on them later.

These crabs also feed on Muscles and shrimp and can be found at depths of around 2,200 meters.

It lives in some of the toughest underwater conditions known to life which happens to be in blistering-hot, sulphurous waters that erupt from the sea bed below.

21. STONEFISH

The Stonefish is the most venomous fish in the world and can be found in the Indian and Pacific oceans. It likes to lay buried deep in the sand waiting for its prey.

It can grow up to 20 inches in length and is covered with different color areas of skin with a specific texture to make it blend with its environment. Stonefish venom can cause severe pain, paralysis and even heart failure. Its poison is very powerful.

It likes to eat various types of fish and shrimps and hunts its prey by waiting patiently and then swallowing its victim super-fast!

Stonefish are able to survive 24 hours outside the water and can live for up to 10 years.

22. GIANT ISOPOD

The Giant Isopod looks kind of creepy but it is not a huge underwater bug. It is a crustacean that is closely related to other sea dwellers like shrimp and crabs.

They can be found as deep as 7000 feet and like to burrow into the sea floor mud or clay for shelter. Typically, their length will be up to 15 inches but there are some bigger ones out there too.

Giant Isopods have four sets of jaws which cut into their prey. They are scavengers and feast on dead animals that fall from the sea surface. They also have two sets of antennae that they use to feel and sense their way around the sea bed.

If an Isopod is threatened by another sea creature it will curl up into a little ball to protect itself from harm. These bug-like creatures live in the Pacific Ocean.

23. LONG-NOSED CHIMAERA

The Long-Nosed Chimaera is different from the average fish because its skeleton is made of cartilage instead of bone.

They have slimy brown and gray scale less skin and have a venomous sharp fin on its back used to defend itself. It also has a long and tapering paddle-shaped snout. This snout has sensitive nerve endings which help the Chimaera find food.

Chimaera can be up to 5 feet in length and have sharp rodent-like teeth in its jaws. They can be found in tropical oceans all around the world and swim to depths of 6,500 feet.

They like to eat shrimp, crabs and other small fish. The female Chimaera lays eggs and these eggs are leathery and horn shaped. We call them by different names such as ratfish, big spine spookfish, rabbitfish and ghost sharks.

24. FRILLED SHARK

The Frilled Shark looks like a big Eel with its sharp teeth, lizard-like head, long slim body and tiny fins. It can grow up to 6.5 feet, (2 metres) and tends to stay in the deep waters of the ocean.

They can swim to depths of 400 to 4,200 feet, (120 to 1,280 metres) although they have been known to go much deeper. They swim around like an Eel by wriggling their long back tails.

The Frilled Shark has a large mouth with around 300 teeth in total along the upper and lower jaw. They eat smaller sharks, tiny fishes, small squid and other tiny creatures.

Its name comes from the six large gills that protrude from just below the side of its head. It captures its prey by lunging forward like a snake.

25. FLABBY WHALEFISH

The Flabby Whale fish is a deep sea creature that resembles a miniature whale. It is one of the deepest-dwelling animals on Earth and swims to depths of over 3500m, (11,500 ft).

These fish have no scales but do have thin, lose or "flabby" skin. They are not huge animals only reaching a length of around 16 inches.

The skin of the Flabby Whale fish is red because red light is not easy to see in the deep ocean. We can see them outside of the water but when they are in the water they literally become invisible because of the surrounding darkness.

They have a set of sensory pores along their body that can detect vibrations in the water. This helps it to navigate and hunt in the darkness.

Check Out My Other Books

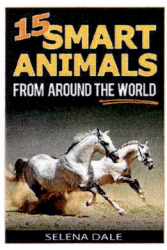  

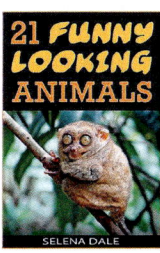 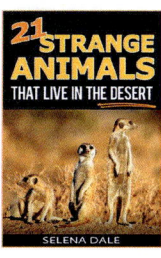 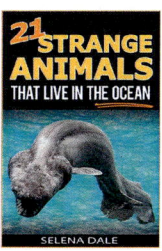

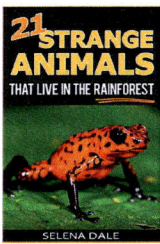  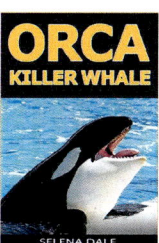

Clink this link to go check out the many books available in this series:

amazon.com/author/selenadale

Or visit:

www.selenadale.com

COLORING BOOKS WONDERLAND COLLECTION

MORE COLORING BOOKS!

CHECK OUT ALL THE LATEST COLORING BOOKS FOR GROWN UPS AND KIDS:

GO TO
www.selenadale.com/coloring-books-wonderland

SUDOKU BOOKS

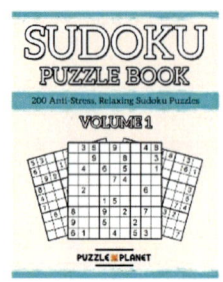 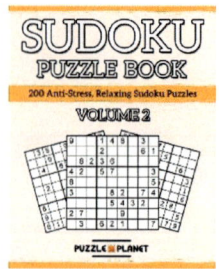 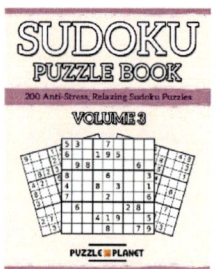

GO TO

www.selenadale.com/puzzle-planet

MORE COLORING BOOKS

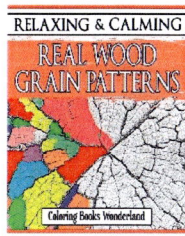  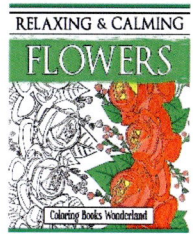

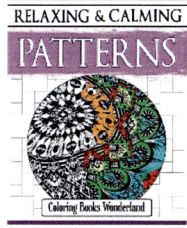 

GO TO

www.selenadale.com/coloring-books-wonderland

DO YOU LIKE
ROMANCE BOOKS?

MANY MORE FUN CHILDREN'S BOOKS COMING SOON!

TO GET YOUR FREE GIFTS

GO TO

www.selenadale.com/get-your-free-gifts

About Selena

Selena Dale was born in United Kingdom, London and has lived there most of her life. She has a passion for writing and loves to learn new things, especially if she can share what she has learned with her two children.

Due to her varied interests and love of writing she decided to create children's books. She can now pick and choose any topic to write about while sharing what she has written with her kids.

"Young children's brains are like sponges, ready to absorb all that wonderful knowledge. A child who loves to read is a child whose imagination will be flexed like a muscle. Now that is a pretty good foundation."

Selena Dale

IMAGE SOURCES

GIANT SQUID
www.deepseanews.com
VIPERFISH
www.thezt2roundtable.com
VAMPIRE SQUID
www.cultnoise.com
HATCHETFISH
www.wikipedia.org
COFFINFISH
www.beach-ness.com
BLUE-RINGED OCTOPUSS
www.theherald.com.au
GIANT SPIDER CRAB
www.stuffpoint.com
BARRWLEYE FISH
www.thegulfblog.com
GRENADIER
www.commons.wikimedia.org
DUMBO OCTOPUSS
www.grindtv.com
BLACK SWALLOWER
www.discoverychannel.com.au
FROGFISH
www.frogfish.ch
LONG NOSED CHIMAERA
www.creepyanimals.com

41440799R00027

Made in the USA
Middletown, DE
13 March 2017